THE ORANGE TREE

PHOENIX POETS

Edited by Srikanth Reddy

The Orange Tree

DONG LI
With a Foreword by Srikanth Reddy

THE UNIVERSITY OF CHICAGO PRESS
CHICAGO & LONDON

The University of Chicago Press, Chicago 60637
The University of Chicago Press, Ltd., London
©2023 by The University of Chicago

Published 2023
Printed in the United States of America

32 31 30 29 28 27 26 25 24 23   1 2 3 4 5

ISBN-13: 978-0-226-82616-5 (paper)
ISBN-13: 978-0-226-82617-2 (e-book)
DOI: https://doi.org/10.7208/chicago/9780226826172.001.0001

Library of Congress Cataloging-in-Publication Data

Names: Li, Dong, 1984- author. | Reddy, Srikanth, 1973- writer of foreword.
Title: The orange tree / Dong Li ; with a foreword by Srikanth Reddy.
Other titles: Phoenix poets.
Description: Chicago : The University of Chicago Press, 2023. | Series: Phoenix poets
Identifiers: LCCN 2022041376 | ISBN 9780226826165 (paperback) | ISBN 9780226826172 (ebook)
Subjects: LCGFT: Poetry.
Classification: LCC PS3612.I134 O73 2023 | DDC 811/.6—dc23/eng/20220909
LC record available at https://lccn.loc.gov/2022041376

♾ This paper meets the requirements of ANSI/NISO Z39.48-1992 (Permanence of Paper).

In memory of C. D.

CONTENTS

Foreword: Srikanth Reddy ix

Aviary of Water and Fire 3
The Orange Tree 13
Live, by Lightning 23
The Army Dreamer 45
The Maple Bridge 67

Glossary: In Search of Words 81
Acknowledgments 83

Some books introduce us to a writer. Some introduce us to a world. Dong Li's *The Orange Tree* is both kinds of book, and it begins, as it must, with an introduction to language itself:

> the longdead
> the griefwall
> the springautumn
> the flightwest

Some Western readers may puzzle over the foreign character in the margin. What is this language? Even if we recognize it as Chinese, we may remain in doubt about its meaning. Are these calligraphic brushstrokes a translation of *longdead*, or *griefwall*, or *springautumn*, or *flightwest*, or none of the above? What's more, we may ask ourselves, what *is* a griefwall? Or springautumn? What is a feeling, or a thing, or a season? What is a word? A world?

A Chinese reader will recognize this cursive figure as the word for water. *The Orange Tree* may decline to translate its Chinese characters into English, but it makes Li's *longdead*, his *griefwall*, his *springautumn*, and his *flightwest* all luminously legible to thought and feeling. Li's book is a family history, which, we learn, is also a history of modern China. To write this history, the poet adopts the literary persona of a wise and innocent child exploring the memory palace of ancestry:

> Winter comes and goes.
> Oranges fall and grow.
> The dead and the living travel through the house.
> Past the shade of the old orange tree.

The measured stateliness of this verse brings to mind the elemental beauty of an exercise in English composition. The English of *The Orange Tree* is a *learned* language of migration, adaptation, and survival. Yet the most common English pronoun, *I*, rarely appears in Li's lexicon, and only in association with the longdead of the book's opening: "Am I dead or dying. / Is death the only family." This requiem in elementary English chronicles the passage of individuals, families, communities, and populations through the griefwall of history into a springautumn beyond chronological time. The compound words of *The Orange Tree*, then, provide the key to a grammar—or is it a metaphysics?—where one is always already both living and dead, present and past, contemporary and historical, a spectral citizen of compound worlds. "[S]he crosses bridge from longing river to grief lake," writes Li, "she has been dead for a long time // maple bridge going a long time."

Like the classic Chinese novels *Romance of the Three Kingdoms* or *Dream of the Red Chamber*, Li's book tells the story not of the one but of the many. The opening invocation, "Aviary of Water and Fire," plucks the *pipa* (Chinese lute) that will accompany *The Orange Tree*'s orchestrated narratives. The book's title poem then introduces us to the child narrator, who will recount his family's history, interwoven with the political history of the People's Republic of China. The next section, "Live, by Lightning," chronicles the stories of the men in Li's family who leave for the Korean War and return, wounded inside and outside, to their communities along the Yangtze and its delta. "The Army Dreamer" chronicles the Li women's flight from the Nanjing Massacre under Japanese occupation, their economic migration to autonomous regions on the peripheries of the new nation, and their return to homes transformed by the Great Leap Forward and the Cultural Revolution. And in "The Maple Bridge," an old uncle and a rebellious aunt are reunited in Li's hometown of Suzhou, against the backdrop of the Hanshan Temple, the Tiger Hill Pagoda, and the legendary Maple Bridge. These longdead bear witness to unimaginable violence— "Screaming was heard, eventually"—and to the expansive intimacies of their world: "the river came from a high place / they could taste the ice in it." Telling their stories in an adopted language, Li's narrator discovers a form of literary dwelling beyond citizenship, ideology, or other forms of cultural belonging. Thus, *The Orange Tree* ends, as it must, with a glossary, "In Search of Words," that offers new expressive registers for "the hellboundhappiness" of humankind.

Only a poet who has traversed more than one world could write such a devastating and luminous book. Born in Suzhou, China, and educated at Deep Springs College and Brown University in the US, Li now lives in Leipzig, Germany, where he translates Chinese, English, French, and German literature. Is he an Anglophone Asian poet, a transnational author, a voice of the Chinese diaspora, or none of the above? The anonymous narrator of *The Orange Tree* may be a literary persona—a self-fashioned poet versed in multiple literary traditions—but he is also Dong Li himself, a collision of water and fire, spring and autumn, innocence and wisdom. It is an honor to introduce this extraordinary book to the world as the recipient of the inaugural Phoenix Emerging Poet Book Prize for 2023.

THE ORANGE TREE

the longdead

the griefwall

the springautumn

the flightwest

the familyfire

the slantingwheels

the departingface

the whirlingdarkness

the wordlesslight

AVIARY

OF

WATER

AND

FIRE

The Chinese say: Woman, water. Man, fire.
Water and flame, they fight.
Wolf she cries to the Great Wall. Tide rises. Slow.
His mind afire on the Long River.
Ready to cross.

Women were water, when the march was not long, when grief held.

Under the rubble of an eight-hundred-mile wall.

She held his cold bones to her warm body.

A lament felled the Great Wall.

Their wedding night was not long ago, a long march away from home.

Then he was forced to build the wall.

Sent before the night of their union.

When spring and autumn clashed in the Middle Kingdom.

The first emperor, Qin Shi Huang, rose to unification before Christ.

Walls were rebuilt against northern tribes playing *pipa* by the prairie bonfire.

She drowned herself in the eastern sea.

Her husband buried under the wall.

Her *pipa* left by the water.

Before dying, the emperor brought his Terracotta Army under Mount Li.

Then the northern tribes broke across the wall.

Great-Grandparents took flight westward.

Before four walls without a roof, before history turns vaguely gray.

Only *pipa* remains to be plucked.

Water, the Way

The Way water floods rice fields in spring.
The Way rice shot sky-high in paddies through Spring and Autumn.
Laozi flew westward on a crane of immortality.
Qin Shi Huang burned books to unify people in the first kingdom that lasted.
Confucius's followers stayed in cities where they were buried alive in ditches.
They chose to live and think.
What is the moral, when the pillow is empty, when the person is dead?
What is the Way?
The Chinese choose to live.
Life passes onto life, name onto name.
Death, you have to find out for yourself.
Bear witness, eastern waters.

The Wheels, the Wheels

Time rolls out a scroll of a few strokes
Spring and autumn slant to history

The self advances toward delusion
Ten thousand things advance to enlightenment

What will trickle, what will drill through
Traveling in the feathering bluebirds

Life departs the face
Genealogy begins to pray

In the new vernacular

In the aviary of

Maternal Great-Grandparents have been dead for a long time.
Paternal Great-Grandparents too.
Maternal Grandparents are long dead. Paternal Grandparents died.
Grandma. Grandpa. You are dead.
Parents are dying. Ma. Fa. You are dying.
Am I dead or dying.
Is death the only family.

Pluck
The
Pipa
The
Great
Wall
Of
Grief
Will
Fall

Pluck
The
Pipa
The
Great
Wall
Of
Grief
Will
Fall

the yellowedphoto

the travelingblood

the oustedgrace

the deadwinter

the ardentbetrayal

the hangingwindow

the streetfight

the wastedwanderer

the burningwhite

THE ORANGE TREE

In a yellowed family photo, there is an orange tree, leaves burned.

The oranges are green, but we are already starting to look alike in the photo.

By the orange tree is Grandparents' house.

We all once walked over its threshold to pick oranges.

The tree was tall, and only men in the family could reach.

Uncle, Grandma's only surviving son, was young then.

He could not reach.

So we took turns to shake the tree.

There is always traveling in the family.

In our blood.

The big orange tree bloomed when Grandparents passed away.

The house was handed over to Uncle.

Next time the oranges turned orange, we would meet again under their shade.

We agreed, just like the times when Grandparents were alive.

Grandpa was born into a general's family in Nanjing.

His father was an ardent follower of Sun Yat-sen.

The eldest son of the family, Grandpa inherited his father's title.

He worked for the Nationalist government of Kuomintang, which Sun founded.

He also took care of the family orchard garden.

In the garden, each generation planted their own orange tree.

During festive times and even in later war times, neighbors were invited.

In the garden, they could enjoy the delicacy of the season.

Grandpa had three brothers and two sisters.

His youngest brother fell in love with a Japanese lady, and they secretly married.

Great-Grandpa ousted him from the family.

We never had orange parties again.

The youngest brother soon got a job as a chauffeur for the Japanese war generals.

He started his own family with the lady.

He became a traitor.

In the dead winter of 1937, Grandpa's orange trees were still in their prime.

The oranges fell at night, one after another, soft on the ground.

The Japanese army invaded the old capital.

In six weeks, three hundred thousand people were tortured.

Buried and burned alive in ditches.

The Yangtze River bloomed orange-red.

Great-Grandpa was able to make some arrangements before the invasion.

He gave all to the Communist Party.

And betrayed Kuomintang.

He arranged for Grandpa to leave for Suzhou.

On December 8, he hanged himself by the window.

The lacquered window opened to the garden of green and red oranges.

The oranges had their first frost.

Before fleeing, Great-Grandpa gave Grandma an orange tree plant.

He told her to plant it where the soil was rich.

When the orange tree was with us, then we would be together.

We would have some shade and fruit in the family.

Soon the two younger brothers were shocked to death.

In anticipation of the atrocities to come and revenge for the fugitives.

The two sisters were reluctant to leave Nanjing.

At a nunnery in the eastern suburb, they shaved their heads.

Grandpa, together with Grandma and their first daughter, fled.

They walked forty-five miles and settled at Rainbow Street 12.

The orange plant was finally put in the soil.

When the family was still in Nanjing, in the family garden.

Maternal Great-Grandparents were having orange parties.

Paternal Great-Grandparents joined the People's Liberation Army on the Long March.

Eighty thousand people went on the march, and seven thousand made it.

To Yan'an Headquarters.

Great-Grandparents were left unburied.

On the firm snowy mountains.

Ten years later, Grandpa joined the party and was later transferred to Suzhou.

In due season, the orange plant bloomed.

Paternal Grandpa liked eating oranges.

Maternal Grandparents held orange parties.

Just like the parties Great-Grandparents held in the family garden.

They met, and Paternal Grandpa became a family friend.

This was just before the founding of the People's Republic of China.

The local Communist Party factions were still fighting for power.

Grandpa was wounded in a street fight.

He dragged his bleeding legs and elbowed his way to Maternal Grandparents' house.

Grandma had some medical knowledge from her surgeon father.

She treated locals for free.

Paternal Grandpa hid under the orange tree until he could walk again.

He was made hero of the party.

He protected Maternal Grandparents' family from execution.

He never mentioned their affiliations.

Day by day, the orange tree grew taller.

But the family never had time to enjoy its fruit or shade.

They recited Chairman Mao's Little Red Book.

The Cultural Revolution began, following Three Years of Natural Disasters.

Mother was four.

She survived famine on orange peels.

Thirty-eight million people died from hunger.

Grandma's first son died of TB.

On her shabby medical table, Grandma died a week later from exhaustion.

Ten years of Cultural Revolution.

Father joined the Red Guards.

At school, they tortured his teachers.

They traveled across the country to meet other young activists.

To propagate Mao's thought.

On a train to Beijing, Father brought a basket of bright-red oranges.

He wanted to see Mao.

Tiananmen Tower was flooded with the orange-red faces of the young guards.

People wandered and wasted away.

They had no time for orange parties.

More orange trees were planted after the Cultural Revolution.

They were no longer a rare delicacy, and more varieties appeared in the marketplace.

After China's Opening, we never had time to meet again at Uncle's house.

Uncle moved into a modern apartment building.

And no one ever picked oranges again.

Still the orange tree bore fruit.

Winter comes and goes.

Oranges fall and grow.

The dead and the living travel through the house.

Past the shade of the old orange tree.

Its white flowers bloom and wilt, then the oranges turn red.

Every year the orange tree turns red.

Grandparents never ate any oranges.

Last year the orange tree suffered from warm weather.

All its leaves were burned white.

the shiftingworlds

the ravishedeardrums

the grindingriver

the shiveringbreath

the lulledrelicsurface

the ghostlitblack

the flurriedwinter

the bloodyabyssfire

the weightlessrivenlightning

LIVE

,

BY

LIGHTNING

Shifting worlds the Yangtze meanders
      from the glaciers of the Tanggula on the Tibetan Plateau
rising and falling Three Gorges and Twelve Peaks
      hanging coffins and cliff carvings names passing
turning and not turning a swift brushstroke easterly to sea
      the river widens the delta flourishes
wind flashes through rice fields into littered houses

                                              Opening

Living on the left bank he listened to boatman songs
        rice crops transported upstream migrating birds far and few
steamboats scared off birdsongs birds never stayed
        but passed his house on their way south from north
thin layers of ice formed on the river and rubbed off
        reminding him of holding hands rushing through a rice field
of sprinkler rippled goose bumps in a flush of a slow flood in spring
        arms and thighs trembling roar of river ravished eardrums
so he looked in tranquil season to the river
        that rolled patiently like a hand about to touch
the river spun into livelihoods of those on the banks
        folded into thickening skin and speckles of red poppies
out of his house he went into his day
        girls beat laundry on the river's banks
their crisp laughter drowned the river that hit the rocks in its way
        water splashed onto their pink-tinted faces
sun left a healthy color yet tanning was rare
        rice steam whitened their cheeks in early evenings
cooking smoke gave wind a shape
        sleeves rolled up he would watch and imagine
staring into clouds until stars pierced through
        then he walked the same quarter of a mile to his house
that would take him along to the grinding days of the river

The river rasped by and slid into the opening of his mind
he would join his river friends in a dark-green truck waiting
to the right bank he would swim across
the river now in the foreground in his mind

One after another his grandparents died
        he spread half of their ashes into the river
into the unknown regions of the river's beds
        they taught him about the river
never thought of leaving the river
        this is where they were
and who they had always been
        no traveler brought a good name to the family
their brick house stood its ground
        through storms and lightning cold sometimes leaked
through thatched roof smelling of the river's grass
        the other half of their ashes he spread into rice fields
his grandparents were rice peasants
        they could tell the weather by breathing the air
the river told them they said it protected them
        the river came from a high place
they could taste the ice in it
        so they let in the river to irrigate rice fields and now
it was their turn
        now he was about to travel

From left to right bank his childhood friends waved
     girls on the left bank watched
flinging himself ashore he would be traveling
     morning fog hid the river's voice
tide drew out the moon behind clouds
     gray of the clouds loomed in the river
sitting on the river's bank he looked past rice fields
     tide reached his feet
his body shivered
     so he stood up and walked home
thinking tired him
     and the moon was too bright
a door shut behind him
     and he walked into night
he could hear his breathing
     in the breath he was already there

{She carried rocks and twigs to fill the sea, the sacred bird.}
{Her beak sharpened by fire on water.}
{She lived upland with her father by the Yellow River.}
{The clans and tribes under his wings.}
{Running after her cry, he slept by the bonfire lit by his people.}
{The river does not run dry.}
{The plateau cracks their flames.}
{Bays curve.}
{Eastern waters.}
{Relics surface.}

Outside the long pavilion by the ancient route, grass greens to the edge of sky.

Listening

Time sinks in the river
he could be dead
was he already memory

New memory took over. Old memory rusted. Would new memory last. His journey entered day. He had to leave. No choice. No regrets. The rice field flooded. The truck bumped. The road was rough. He lowered his head. Watching was dizzying. Old friends went silent. He sat in the roar of the river on a long ride. The parting was not difficult. He was still himself. He looked at his hands.

Lay down your weathered body. Fierce winter. Sun flurries clouds.

Listen:

the Yalu River roars
from the glaciers of the Paektu
Mountain to the Yellow Sea
wave of skin
shield of blood
gushing
to sterilize
hill country
wind howled
through rice fields
sweeping husks
over

Triangle Hill Sniper Ridge
rubbing off a V shape
under lush green cover
tunnels trenches dug beneath
obstacles erected along minefields
peace talk sank to silences
bloodbath

the Battle of Triangle Hill
watering down bare ridges

on the left bank Volunteer Army
shuttled through tunnels
on the right bank UN bombers faced forces
on a flinty morning
foliage seared in smoke
fortifications on fire
Volunteer Army in the bluing
dark

breathe
heads down
tunnel troops crouched
blood hardened in the cold
bayonets drawn in and out
hand to hand
flares ripped the bombing veil
rocks thrown kept the wave
rolling
artillery blanketed ground
march
skin peeled
skin

UN forces took Volunteer Army for ghosts
eyes blade bright
sharpening in veins
bloody abyss of flameless fire

then looking
pierced
charred sky
birds still

stand
and
burn

In the middle of the river his body bloated in bald winter
on the left bank his country blazed in the blue hour before daybreak
on the right bank Goguryeo relics bombed clean
the Yalu rushed and washed clumps of surfaced bodies
days into nights nights onto days drilled and chilled in bones
from north to south and backward his blood boiled mind melting
he stayed still sipping a reed straw bobbing softly above
in slow motion trucks bumped across bombers
in shadows of rain skin waffled by water
heavy hails of bullets skimmed mutely
eyelids flipped by the glint of first light

Everybody carried fire. It was a long time. Spring flood. All quiet.
Rice grows in water and shoots into sky.

You are again. In the middle of the river. You could turn now. Turn.
Do you see your house. Do you hear the laughter of river girls.
Do not weep. They could not see you. In the water. You would be fine.
Fine weather dangled on a sunset. Night opening.
The requiem drew breath.
You are ready. Stars pop on the horizon. You would not see them.
Past a sheet of bullet rain. Rice crops laid down their hulls.
Pull your cramped leg. Do not breathe. They would find you.

Shot in his kidney and transferred to a rear troop. Survived three days in the bloody river. Most of his comrades were dead. His mind was never clear again. In the military hospital he slept for days. When he heard birds passing through night, he would turn to the light and throw anything he could reach at the ceiling. She was waiting for him. Across the Yalu River. Across the Yellow River. Across the Yangtze River. His girl child faltered in his mind. He would never stand up again.

weightless

a cargo train crosses a night
bridge a catwalk
board beneath a track
windows pass
a strange
face flies through fine silhouette

Woke up. Bed shaking. Not in wind. Train rattled. Tracks crushed solid. Fields passed him through the window. So did time. He thought. Crossing again. Then black. Then silence. Not even the cargo train made a singular sound. All the screaming. Only beginning. In the dark. A messy evening of stars. The mindscape started on horse engine, coal fueled, manual crank. Escape. Their faces. Dying. His old boots. His hands. Riven. By lightning.

the drifteddream

the snowsoakedgarden

the anguishednight

the shreddeddays

the augustwoman

the shufflingthreshold

the farawayorangetree

the dwindledwhispers

the launderedyears

THE

ARMY

DREAMER

Tell Our Daughters (Besmilr Brigham)

Lilac, a Requiem

July, late snow. July, lilacs not yet bloomed in full. Day began as usual. Coyotes howled as if it were night. A dog bark, then another. All the dogs barking. Dogs could not venture out last night. Rice bushels peasants gathered wasted in their courtyards. There was some shuffling in the snow.

facing the snow, lilac up the ragged road

No one knew how many roads she had walked before this. No one knew how many bridges she had crossed before summer. No one knew her, and it had snowed. Wiping off the snow, she dug her face into the bushels. They smelled of summer. The bushels were frozen, and so was her face. It was as if time had frozen and whitened into snow. In the snow her long dress looked purple. She always wore a purple dress, no matter the season. Something she had kept for years. When summer never snowed. When it always summered. Her feet purpled. The dogs stopped barking. They were chewing on her bones. She was covered in snow. From some distance, the edge of her dress. Her mind started to drift until it reached purple. Then her eyes opened. She saw summer coming.

down the ragged road, lilacs snow

The first time she was allowed to stroll in the garden, it was summer. Lilacs had already bloomed. Their petals purpled the garden. She collected lilacs and brewed tea out of them. Then she put on a lilac dress. She met her first man and her many men. She felt nothing. The blood that flowed from her purpled and paled. Purple in flood. Snow thawed. Her body stiffened. Like a tree. On that morning no light was turned. She heard lilacs blooming. She has been dead for a long time. Purple lilac her only friend. Deep in the rice bushels, her body. Her mind frozen, lilac came to a stall. Driftless bird, a song.

facing the snow, lilac up the ragged road
down the ragged road, lilacs snow

Event

imagine the smell
of kudzu, imagine that
kudzu has a smell
myopic edge of night
imagine the impression
of an object, imagine that
object has an impression
swollen hands slowly
over belly
imagine the dream
of birth, imagine that
birth is dream-
like insides
imagine the kick
of a rib, a scent of rubber
just whistle

Last night. It snowed. The garden a mess. Flakes drifted into her dream. Screaming was heard, eventually. Wrapped in cotton. By the stove. Light was turned on that morning. She opened her eyes to a world she saw for the first time. She shook. Her parents trembled in the fleeting air. Some steps in the snow-soaked garden. Disappearing. Covered.

day slides against night anguish time shredding the mind
when her parents grabbed her hand to leave the family
garden she screamed their hands were heavy weighing on
the throat like a tub of water everything poured

a chain of events a single catastrophe wreckage upon
wreckage before her bare feet dead logs of bodies floated
and lapped against the long shores of the yangtze north of
nanjing more bodies burned in dripping fat men women
young old

someone stood up from the ditch and tore up his smeared
white shirt a white flag waved japanese soldiers signaled
him to jump back his hands behind his head he waited and
looked up

thirty japanese soldiers broke into his house he opened
the door holes from head to toe they shot him his
neighbor dropped his knees on the ground and begged
they shot him and stomped on his bones the wife of
the first man was hiding under the table with a one year
old in her arms they dragged her out snatched her baby
screaming they chopped the baby up started a fire ready to
grill in the yard the mother gang raped her breasts sheared
off a beer bottle in her vagina

five japanese soldiers flung themselves into a room a
father and two daughters were having porridge gone bad
the smell forced the soldiers to hold their noses bowls
dropped jaws opened they bound the father to a chair
gang raped his teenage daughters before him inserted
bundles of chopsticks into their vaginas hammering them
in with bayonets then hacked off their heads and smashed
their brains on his face

a fifteen year old girl sought shelter in an american
school in the safe zone carrying her six month old child
a japanese soldier teased his bayonet on her buttocks she
spit he stabbed her slit open her belly at a bloody lump he
yelled

someone jumped into the river with his brother japanese
soldiers threw grenades his brother shredded to pieces he
floated on these body parts under the cover of night when
the soldiers were gone he swam ashore leaving pieces of
his brother behind he took clothes off a headless man and
put them on found his way to the nunnery under the roof
in the eastern city the nuns gave him a rice bowl

in a neighboring village four brothers ran a farm japanese
soldiers found them put the eldest in a canvas bag and
ordered the other three to set fire in a well they sank the
latter dumped the charred bag and lit cigarettes

inside the city walls people were driven to the central
square with bayonets and rifles japanese soldiers stripped
them whipped them to crawl on top of each other drove
their tanks back and forth left and right until the ground
flattened dragged out those still alive and forced them to
dig a big ditch and throw in their dead the alive piled hay
then threw themselves into the ditch

she felt quiet the city intact for six dynasties a relic she
looked away fixtures and fittings of everything rags and
rubbles rough stones naked beams shattered masonry
inaudible invisible washing off the fatigue of days no
question of botany no grass not a blade in sight upon days
parcels and sacks crates and cartons shoulders bent under
their burdens people looked small no eyes could be seen

the world shifts the yangtze meanders people were
sleeping she did not look she would fly them to foreign
shores then storm fired in the back of her mind bluing
candlelit like ghosts like ravens like something flying back
into night

{she was caught up}
{days}
{pushed to walk the long road}
{before her}
{the walk}
{they were flying}
{skyward}
{river to shore}
{like ghosts}
{like ravens}
{like something flying back}
{into night}
{look away}
{no shade out of darkness}
{there was no time}
{to think}
{to act}
{time shreds}
{she was flying jellyfish like}
{no difference}
{float}
{lightly}
{lighter}
{lightest}

This morning. She faces her. Shadow. Lonely.
Before knowing.

the army dreamer

the river rolled patiently

                               the crossing ceased quietly

she would gaze for hours beating clothes on the bank

                                     warily her years

if she spilled soup on the table she had to stand in the courtyard

                     she would fall asleep against lichened walls

she stole identity papers from the family wardrobe

                           the threshold crossed

no turning back

                    family disappearing in her mind

her travels her

                          life was to begin

no traveler brought a good name to the family

                a dark green truck was waiting for her

started on horse engine

                    noise overriding the river

falling prey to winter

                she startled in the back of the truck

the dark gray fabric illuminated by the moon

                    waning inside herself

complete darkness of the interior

    the orange tree in the family courtyard shined through frost

her mind went black

oranges dropped in the faraway orchard

a light turned on

                                        she would cross the river

join the army

                                        she was not married off

she was free

                        behind her ears she thought of happiness

from yangtze river to yellow plateau

a loose strand of hair

an owl asleep on the stiff branch

she went away

eventually

crossing quietly

the maid of honor has been dead for a long time

bones picked by birds

                in whipping sandstorms

only teeth glittered

                when light shone

when rain

              she was crossing

the dry river

              the grass high

sheep flashed over the paling moon

              she was ready

the emperor saw her off

              marriage sealed her red veil

she joined the hunnic parade against the picking wind

            her hunnic husband was by her side

he built her a yurt in a faraway place

the han dynasty receded into unnamed graveyards outside the wall

the han emperor died a year after she was gone

        she died sixty years before dynasty crumbled to ashes

before barbarians tore apart the great wall

                                                            come
easy to come

                                                   go so difficult
to go

                                    years laundered in the long long river
easy to part

                                             difficult to see you again
grief of love and hate runs deep in the grain

                              whispers dwindled between sand and stars
outside the wall

                                                  smell of tumbleweeds
long pavilion by the ancient route

                                        grass green to the edge of sky
wind fingered willows

                                                        flute died out
sunset mountain over mountain

                                            the han dynasty went under
the huns crossed the yin mountains

                             the maid of honor has been dead for a long time
she could not find her step in the river

as she herded sheep and meshed with grass
her sister was sent north to plant rice
up to the mountains down to the villages
mao slogans flapped in her face
she also joined the army
shaved her head dumped her hair in campfire
her mind never clear again
she dreamed
on a night train
she crossed
shuffled over the threshold
come easy
come

go
so difficult to go
years laundered in the long long river
part easy to part
hard to see you again
grief love and hate run deep in the grain
dead husbands dead parents

the revolution over
the movement over

                                        one way ticket to hell
for parents

                                        happiness
deng opened china
                        the river rolled like a hand about to touch
morning and evening on the far bank
                                        years in the middle
fixate on a point and see

                                        remember
after a long walk
                        from besieged city to river town
she was beaten when the water bucket was not full
                would spend the night with stray dogs in the street
one day she left without moving her hands
                        the threshold still fired in her mind
time past the river

                                        disappearing

divorced

                                     forced

she opened a food stall

                          by the railway station

her legs became strong

                     running away from the police

permitless

                         years rivered on the side

in her mind the threshold still

                           she made ends meet

under a new roof

                 the food stall moved into the station

she hired helping hands

                     fell in love with one of them

never married

                marriage was never in her mind again

she traveled far and foreign

                           rivers and shores

train ride jumped on her

                        she went almost blind

came home

                   her parents dead for a long time

before their graves in the countryside

                          she spit fire

light across the river

                                   flooded the banks

wave of skin shield of blood through bare prairie

                                  wind howled through rice fields

sweeping husks

                                  from river town to hill country

from rice paddies to wheat fields

                                  the crossing again

the crossing never again

                              day slides against the anguish of night

time shredding the mind

                                 fog and rain in the mountains

army dreamer on a white horse

                            a sleeve of twilight pierced the waters

the crowcawsforestfrost

the moonslidesdownriver

the matboatmuteshores

the fishermantorchlight

the daybreaknightanguish

the nightflymaplebridge

the ravenlikeghostfire

the longingrivergrieflake

the hellboundhappiness

THE

MAPLE

BRIDGE

only the crossing counts (C. D. Wright)

```
S        T                    R
L        H                    E
I        E         S          S
D        M         O          O
E        I         U          U
         N         N          N
A        D         D          D
                              
F        O         W
I        N         R
N                  I
G        T         N
E        H         K
R        E         L
                   E
O        G         S
N        U
         Q         T
T        I         H
H        N         E
E                  
                   P          R
G        F         L          I
U        I         A          P
Q        N         Y          P
I        G         I          L
N        E         N          E
         R         G
                   
         T         H
S        H         A
L        E         N
I                  D
D        M
E        I
         N
         D
```

SLIDE A FINGER ON THE GUQIN SLIDE

THE MIND ON THE GUQIN FINGER THE MIND

SOUND WRINKLES THE PLAYING HAND

RESOUND RIPPLE

bell tolls

                                        caws through forest frost
                                     mat boat along mute shores
                               fisherman shuffles behind torchlight
                                     maple bridge hanging in night
                              wooden fish chimes around wooden beams
                                   abbot hanshan mutters incantations

hanshan served and went to war
moved to countryside and picked up hoe
packed some books and wandered along wild banks
stayed in mountains and dreamed in cold
gathered leaves and thatched a hut among pines
dug a pond and led a trickle from brook

                               bamboo gate blended into faraway peaks
                                     years passed on mirror still river
                                 cranes snatched fishes leaping at leisure
                                      rice sown vegetables planted
                                       brook ran restlessly clear

hanshan drifted toward spring
chewed on mushrooms and drank dew
chased hares and vultures
sunbathed on slippery rocks shaded by olive trees

                                              rocks for pillows
                                             opening old sutras
                                             sores in hot spring
                                               smoky vistas
                                            hut creaked in storm
                                             breathing in rain
                                              towering peaks
                                             wandering miles
                                          hell bound to happiness

abbot hanshan has been dead for a long time

bell tolls

tang dynasty poet zhang ji has been dead for a long time
ousted by his emperor and wasted
floated along yangtze and moored
stumbled on rock slates by shore
whisked his wine bottle off silk belt
drank to moon last droplet to river

moon sank rippling against bridge
bottle bobbed in sinking river
breath leaving
river his only friend
maple bridge do you see it all

zhang ji named you and you lived

bell tolls

                                                        crow through forest
                                                             moon down
                                                           mat boat moored
                                                         fisherman shuffles
                                                       maple bridge hanging

        tiger hill creeps in far firelight
        thousand soldiers dyed rocks red
        spring autumn kingdoms sank in a well
        cranes flying south wooden bridges creaking
        maple leaves still red
        face yellowed in river
        rain ravishes her face
        winter sweets bloom
        shaking flower tree
        petals tear through wind
        fleeting air of winter on white breath
                                    the capturers have been dead for a long time
                                    the captured have been dead for a long time
        a long time men are dead
        a long time women are dead

bell tolls

      she crosses bridge from south to north
      at a candy factory she was assigned a job
      gulping down half a pound a day
      nearby taihu lake freezes and joins yangtze

                            she crosses bridge from city to temple
                                orange tree flowers in spring
                                    women pick tea in mist

      she crosses bridge from garden to town
      lotus riots in pond
      pipa plucked lantern riddles from mouth to mouth

                                she crosses bridge from boat
                                    twenty moons under
                              tea olives run rampant in garden
                              schoolchildren turn in circles

      she crosses bridge from blue mountain to green river
      opening a window
      knitting a sweater under an orange lamp

                      she crosses bridge from longing river to grief lake
                              she has been dead for a long time

      maple bridge going a long time

toll bells

    slant yunyan pagoda on tiger hill
    sink armies in whirling blood storm
    hack off his knees and gouge out his eyes
    pull his body in four directions on horse engine
    bring home all his parts
    fill yangtze with his ashes and bones
    let him have his fingers and toes
                                 ghostfire
                                     ravenlike
                                          flying

    like you

when you die
       i would be a night cloud

when you die
       river flood in spring

when you die
       i would shine down bluebirds

when you die
       fire on distant islands

when you die
       i would be your rice field

                                        she said

                                           death

                                   drown yourself

on his shoulders his comrade carried him home she saw his face he did not look up he was asleep far away from everything his comrade bit his lower lip she held out her hands and turned his face toward her she was ready to carry him threshold rivered her spine bent she smelled something like fire slowed step by step she sat him in a big wooden pail no faucet water boiled pail after pail she poured his boots she lifted his overcoat held close to cheek she dropped everything were tanks coming rubbed his shoulder with a worn sponge of dried gourd native to delta dirt would come off in water so would his mind he was coming back to her in warm water slowly cooling steam watered her face he pointed to his overcoat from front pocket she fished out a yellowed photo he said yalu river where he crossed she looked and foreign shores in steamed air fluttered and settled on water her face under her hands he tried to reach her so far away he was night covering their eyes it was late

in the yellowed photo his hand on a pail her hand warm to touch like a caress on river
but their hands were naked and across them hisses a white horse

when
it
is
time

you
cross
that
bridge

as
you
cross
a
welter
of
bridges

and

you
are
there

as
you
are

you
leave

nothing
behind

and
it
is
becoming

GLOSSARY

in search of words

the longdead

the griefwall

the springautumn

the flightwest

the familyfire

the slantingwheels

the departingface

the whirlingdarkness

the wordlesslight

the yellowedphoto

the travelingblood

the oustedgrace

the deadwinter

the ardentbetrayal

the hangingwindow

the streetfight

the wastedwanderer

the burningwhite

the shiftingworlds

the ravishedeardrums

the grindingriver

the shiveringbreath

the lulledrelicsurface

the ghostlitblack

the flurriedwinter

the bloodyabyssfire

the weightlessrivenlightning

the drifteddream

the snowsoakedgarden

the anguishednight

the shreddeddays

the augustwoman

the shufflingthreshold

the farawayorangetree

the dwindledwhispers

the launderedyears

the crowcawsforestfrost

the moonslidesdownriver

the matboatmuteshores

the fishermantorchlight

the daybreaknightanguish

the nightflymaplebridge

the ravenlikeghostfire

the longingrivergrieflake

the hellboundhappiness

ACKNOWLEDGMENTS

My gratitude to the editors and readers of the magazines in which part of this work was first published:

Barrow Street: excerpt from "The Maple Bridge"
Cincinnati Review: excerpt from "Live, by Lightning"
Conjunctions: "The Orange Tree"
Denver Quarterly: "In Search of Words"
Fence: "The Army Dreamer" and "Rivers and Foreign Shores"
H.O.W.: "Aviary of Water and Fire"
Plume: "When It Is Time"
Prelude: "Weightless" and "Event"
West Branch: "Lilac, a Requiem" and excerpt from "The Maple Bridge"

I am grateful, too, to the Olive B. O'Connor Fellowship at Colgate University, Millay Arts, Virginia Center for the Creative Arts, Corporation of Yaddo, Kimmel Harding Nelson Center for the Arts, Akademie Schloss Solitude, Camargo Foundation, and Kulturstiftung des Freistaates Sachsen for their generous support at various stages of this project.

My deep gratitude to Xu Jing for her calligraphic characters of water and fire, which animate the book.

Thank you to Srikanth (Chicu) Reddy, along with Rosa Alcalá, Douglas Kearney, and Katie Peterson, for believing in this book. I would like to thank Chicu especially for his illuminating foreword.

Thank you to Alan Thomas for bringing the good news and to David B. Olsen for keeping things in order. Thanks also to the incredible team at the University of Chicago Press that helped to put this book together, including Adriana Smith, Mint Liu, and Adrienne Meyers.

I am indebted to all my family and friends, among whom I owe particular thanks to Katie Peterson for locating my courage in the desert, to Keith and Rosmarie Waldrop for their example, to Peter Balakian for letting me follow my instinct, to Forrest Gander for his abiding friendship, and to Don Mee Choi for pushing me to persist. Thank you to my mother, without whose stories and sacrifices this book would not have found its words.